MW00810387

FIRST
IRISH GRAMMAR

BY

THE CHRISTIAN BROTHERS

DUBLIN

M. H. GILL & SON, O'CONNELL STREET

1906

3275.27.3

✓

HARVARD
UNIVERSITY
LIBRARY

This Compendium of Ⴃɼáıméaɲ ɲɑ Ⴃaeↄıꞁⳤe is intended to meet the wants of young students who require, in a concise form, the salient points of Irish Accidence and Syntax.

The Sections throughout the Compendium are numbered as in the larger Grammar, in order to afford facility of reference to those who may desire to obtain more detailed information on any point.

PART I.

ACCIDENCE.

1. The Irish alphabet contains eighteen letters; the vowels are ᴀ, e, ı, o, u; the consonants, ʙ, c, ᴅ, ꜰ, ᴢ, ʜ, ʟ, m, n, p, ꞃ, ꞃ, ᴛ.

2. ᴀ, o, u are called **broad** vowels; e and ı are called **slender** vowels.

The vowels may be either **long** or **short.** The long vowels are marked by means of a ꞃíneᴀᴅ (′) placed over the vowel; *e.g.*, móꞃ, ʙí, mé.

7. An Irish consonant is broad whenever it is beside a broad vowel, in the same word; it is slender when beside a slender vowel.

Aspiration.

15. When we say that an Irish consonant is *aspirated*, we mean that the breath is not completely stopped in the formation of the consonant, and hence the consonantal sound is *continuous*.

16. Aspiration is marked in writing and in print by placing a dot over the consonant aspirated, *e.g.*, ʙ, ċ, ᴅ.

17. In writing, **nine** of the consonants, viz., ᵈ, c, ᵈ, ꜰ, ᵹ, ᵐ, ᵖ, ꞃ, ᵗ, can be aspirated.

Rules for Aspiration of Initial Consonant.

21. (*a*) The **possessive adjectives,** mo, *my* ; ᵈo, *thy* ; and ᴀ, *his,* cause aspiration —mo ᵈó, *my cow.*

(*b*) The **article aspirates** nouns (except those beginning with ᵈ, ᵗ, ꞃ), in the nom. and acc. fem. sing., and in the gen. masc. sing.—ᴀn ᵈeᴀn, *the woman* ; mᴀc ᴀn ꝼiꞃ, (*the*) *son of the man.*

(*c*) In **compound words** the initial consonant of the second word is aspirated, ꞃeᴀn-ṁáᵗᴀiꞃ, *a grandmother.*
The letters ᵈ and ᵗ are never aspirated after a word that ends in one of the letters ᵈ, n, ᵗ, ⅼ, ꞃ.

(*d*) The **interjection** ᴀ, the sign of the voc. case, causes aspiration in nouns of both genders and both numbers—ᴀ Ṡeᴀmᴀiꞃ, (*O*) *James* ; ᴀ ᵈuine, *Sir.*

(*e*) An **adjective is aspirated** when it agrees with a fem. noun in the nom. and acc. sing., or with a masc. noun in the gen. sing., and in the dat. and the voc. sing. of both genders ; also in the nom. and acc. pl.

when the noun ends in a *slender* consonant
—bó bán, *a white cow*; mac an ḟiṁ móiṁ,
(*the*) *son of the big man*; capaill móṁa, *big horses*.

(*g*) A **verb is aspirated**—(1) in the imperfect, the simple past, and the conditional (ordinary forms); (2) after ní, *not*; má, *if*; maṁ, *as*; ṁuṫ (or ṁaṁ) *before*, and all the compounds of ṁo (§ 278); (3) after the relative particle a, *e.g.*, buail ṁé, *he struck*; ní béiṫ ṁé, *he will not be.*

(*h*) The word following ba and baṫ (the past tense and conditional of iṫ) is usually aspirated—ba ṁaiṫ liom, *I liked.*

(*i*) The **simple prepositions** (except aṡ, aṁ, ṡan, ṡo, i, and le) cause aspiration—ṫo ṗáṁaiṡ, ó Ṡeaṫán.

(*j*) The **Numeral adjectives**, aon, *one*; ṫá, *two*; céaṫ, *first*; ṫṁeaṁ, *third*, cause aspiration: ṫá capall, *two horses*; an céaṫ buacaill, *the first boy.*

Eclipsis.

22. Eclipsis is the suppression of the sound of the initial consonant of a word by prefixing another consonant whose sound is substituted.

23. Only **seven** consonants can be eclipsed, viz. : b, c, ṫ, f, ṡ, p, ṫ. Each consonant has its own eclipsing letter.

25. ḃ is eclipsed by m, as a mbó, their cow.

c "	"	" ʒ,	" áɼ ʒcapall, our horse.
ꝺ "	"	" n,	" áɼ nꝺáɲ, our poem.
f "	"	" ḃ,	" ı ḃfuıl, in blood.
ʒ "	"	" nʒ,*	" a nʒé, their goose.
p "	"	" b,	" a bpáıpéaɼ, their paper.
ꞇ "	"	" ꝺ,	" a ꝺꞇaıḃ, their bull.

Rules for Eclipsis.

26. (a) The **possessive adjectives plural**
—áɼ, *our*; buɼ, *your*; a, *their*, cause
eclipsis : a mbáꝺ, *their boat.*

(b) The **article eclipses in the gen.
pl.** (both genders)—lámạ na bfeaɼ, *(the)
hands of the men.*

(c) The **simple prepositions followed
by the article eclipse** the initial of singular
nouns—aɼ an ʒcapall, *on the horse* ; aʒ an
bfeaɼ, *at the man.*

Ꝺo and ꝺe followed by the article *may* aspirate : ꝺo'n
feaɼ, or ꝺo'n ḃfeaɼ, *to the man.*

(d) The **Numeral adjectives** ɼeaċꞇ,
oċꞇ, naoı, and ꝺeıċ (7, 8, 9, 10), and their
compounds 27, 28, &c., cause eclipsis—
ɼeaċꞇ mba, *seven cows.*

(e) The initial of **a verb is eclipsed**
after an, cá, ca (*not*) ʒo, ꝺá, muɲa (muna),
naċ, and the relative a preceded by a

* Only the n is written. See large Grammar on this point.

preposition—cá bfuil ré, *where is he ?* nac
bfuil ré tinn, *is he not sick ?*

Insertion of n, t, and h.

27. (*a*) When a **word begins with a
vowel,** n is prefixed in all positions, in
which a consonant would be eclipsed unless
the preceding word ends in n—áṗ n-aṗán ;
reactt n-aṗail ; but, aṗ an uirce.

(*b*) Prepositions (except do and
de) ending in a vowel prefix n to the
poss. adjs. a (= *his, her, their*), áṗ, buṗ :
le n-a máċaiṗ, *with his mother.*

28. (*a*) The **article prefixes** t to masc.
nouns beginning with a vowel in the nom.
and acc. sing.—an t-aċaiṗ ; an t-aṗal.

(*b*) If a **noun begins with** ṗ followed
by a vowel or by l, n, or ṗ, the article
prefixes t in the nom. and acc. fem. and
the gen. masc. sing.—an tṗúil, *the eye* ; an
tṗṗón, *the nose* ; tiṗ an tṗaṡaiṗt, *the priest's
house.*

(*c*) t is often prefixed to ṗ after
words ending in n : aon tṗúil aṁáin.

29. **Particles which neither aspirate
nor eclipse, and which end in a vowel,**
prefix n to words beginning with a vowel:
e.g., a, *her*, ṡo, le, daṗa (taṗna), ré, tṗí,

ná (*the*, in gen. sing. fem. and in the nom.
acc. and dat. pl.)—ᴀ n-ᴀᴄᴀιη, *her father* ;
ηé n-ᴀηᴀιl, *six asses.*

30. **Attenuation** is the process of making
a broad consonant slender. This is usually
denoted by placing an "ι" immediately
before the consonant: *e.g.,* bᴀη, bᴀιη (*death*).

33. **Syncope** is the elision of an *unac-
cented* vowel or digraph from the last
syllable of a word of *more* than one syllable, whenever the word is lengthened by
an inflection beginning with a *vowel :* *e.g.,*
cοᴅlᴀιm, *I sleep*, from cοᴅᴀιl ; mᴀιᴅne
from mᴀιᴅιn (*morning*).

THE ARTICLE.

37. In Irish there is only *one* article, ᴀn,
which corresponds to the English definite
article, "*the.*" In the singular the form for
all the cases is ᴀn, except the gen. fem.
which is nᴀ. In all the cases of the plural
the form is nᴀ.

39. The prepositions ι, ιn, or ᴀnn, *in*,
le, *with*, take η before the article, *e.g.,* ιnη
ᴀn leᴀbᴀη, *in the book* ; leιη ᴀn bηeᴀη,
with the man.

In Munster ó, ᴅo, and ᴅe, and sometimes others (ᴄηé, ᴀιᴣe, etc.) take η before

the *plural* article—ᴅoᴦ nᴀ ᴃuᴀɪᴅ, *to the cows.*

40. The initial changes produced by the article: Refer to §§ 21 (*b*) ; 26 (*b*), (*c*) ; 28 (*a*), (*b*) ; 29.

THE NOUN.

41. There are only **two** genders in Irish, the masculine and the feminine.

42. Masculine Nouns : (*a*) Names and occupations of males ; (*b*) Personal agents ending in óɪᴩ, ᴀɪᴩe, uɪᴅe or ᴀċ : (*c*) diminutives in ín or ᴀn, and abstract nouns in ᴀᴦ , *d*) Many nouns ending in a *broad* consonant.

43. Feminine Nouns : (*a*) Names and designation of females ; (*b*) Names of countries and rivers ; (*c*) Nouns of two or more syllables ending in ᴀċᴛ or óɢ ; (*d*) Abstract nouns formed from the genitive singular feminine of adjectives ; (*e*) Monosyllabic nouns ending in a *slender* consonant.

44. In Irish there are **five cases**—the Nominative, the Accusative, the Genitive, the Dative (or Prepositional) and the **Vocative.**

52. There are **five declensions** of nouns.
The declensions are distinguished by the
inflection of the genitive singular.

First Declension.

53. All the nouns of the first declension
are masculine, and end in a broad consonant.

54. The genitive sing. is formed by
attenuation § 30; the dat. is the same as
the nom., and the voc. is the same as the
gen. The nom. pl. is the same as the gen.
sing., and the gen. pl. is the same as the
nom. sing.

55. **bᴀ́ᴅ,** *a boat.*

	SINGULAR.	PLURAL.
Nom. & Acc.	bᴀ́ᴅ, a boat	báıᴅ, boats
Gen.	báıᴅ, of a boat	báᴅ, of boats
Dat.	báᴅ, (in) a boat	báᴅᴀıb, (in) boats
Voc.	ᴀ báıᴅ, O boat!	ᴀ báᴅᴀ, O boats!

56. Words of *more than one* syllable
ending in ᴀċ or eᴀċ form their gen. sing.
by changing ᴀċ or eᴀċ into ᴀıᵹ or ıᵹ,
respectively.

60. Vᴏᴡᴇʟ Cʜᴀɴɢᴇs.

Change éᴀ or eu in nom. sing. into éı in gen. sing.

„ o (short) „ „ „ „ uı „ „ „
„ ıo or eᴀ „ „ „ „ ı „ „ „

Change ıᴀ into éı in ıᴀʀc, clıᴀb, nıᴀll, ᵹıᴀll, ʀcıᴀll,
pıᴀċ, and a few others.

SINGULAR.

62. N. & A. mapcac, *rider.* pean, *a man.* cnoc, *a hill.*
GEN. mapcaıᵹ pıp cnuıc
DAT. mapcac peap cnoc
VOC. a ṁapcaıᵹ a ṗıp a cnuıc

PLURAL.

NOM. & ACC. mapcaıᵹ pıp cnuıc
GEN. mapcac peap cnoc
DAT. mapcacaıḃ peapaıḃ cnocaıḃ
VOC. a ṁapcaca a ṗeapa a cnoca

Irregularities in the First Declension.

64. mac, a son; and bıaḋ, food, become mıc and bıḋ in gen. sing.

65. Aonac, a fair; ʋopap, a door; aınᵹeal, an angel; bótap, a road; maʋpaḋ, a dog; plaḃpaḋ, a chain, and mapᵹaḋ, a market, become aoncaıᵹe (or aonaıᵹe), ʋoıppe, aınᵹle, bóıtpe, maʋpaıḋe, plaḃpaıḋe, and mapᵹaıḋe in nom. pl.

66. The following nouns take a in the nom. pl.: bpuac, a brink; caop, a berry; ʋeop, a tear; peann, a pen; peoʋ, a jewel; pméap, a blackberry; uball, an apple (ubla).

67. The following take ca in nom. pl.: peol, a sail; ceol, music; néal, a cloud; pcéal, a story; cuan, a harbour; céaʋ, a hundred; lıon, a net.

Second Declension.

71. All nouns of the second declension end in consonants, and are feminine. The gen. sing. is formed by adding e ; (if the noun ends in a broad consonant, it must

be attenuated § 30), and if the last consonant is c, it is changed into ʒ (except
in words of *one* syllable). The dat. sing. is
got by dropping the e of the gen. The
voc. sing. is like the nom. The nom. pl. is
formed from the nom. sing. by adding ᴀ or
e ; the gen. pl. is like the nom. sing.

78. For vowel changes in gen. sing., refer
to § 60, to which add, ıᴀ becomes éı.

	SINGULAR.		[*woman.*
N. & A.	láṁ, *a hand.*	ʒéaʒ, *a branch.*	caılleaċ, *an old*
GEN.	láiṁe	ʒéıʒe	caıllıʒe
DAT.	láiṁ	ʒéıʒ	caıllıʒ
VOC.	ᴀ láṁ	ᴀ ʒéaʒ	ᴀ ċaılleaċ

	PLURAL.		
N. & A.	láṁa	ʒéaʒa	caılleaċa
GEN.	láṁ	ʒéaʒ	caılleaċ
DAT.	láṁaıḃ	ʒéaʒaıḃ	caılleaċaıḃ
VOC.	ᴀ láṁa	ᴀ ʒéaʒa	ᴀ ċaılleaċa

87. The following nouns take eanna in nom. pl.:—
cúır, a cause ; luıḃ, an herb ; béım, a stroke ; ᴠuaır,
a prize ; léım, a leap ; áıc, a place ; rcoıl, a school ;
céım, a step ; uaır, an hour ; rráıᴠ, a street ; páırc, a
field ; reır, a festival, a feis.

88. The following take eaċa in nom. pl. :—obaır
(oıḃreaċa), a work ; lıcır, a letter ; uḃ, an egg (also
uıḃe) ; paᴠoır, a prayer ; rráıᴠ, a street.

89. The noms. pl. of coıll, a wood ; cír, a coun-
try ; aʒaıᴠ, a face ; rpéar, the sky, are, coıllce,
cíorca, aıʒce, rpéarca.

Third Declension.

91. The third declension includes (1) personal nouns ending in óⁱⱼ or éⁱⱼ (all masculine), (2) derived nouns in ᴀᴄᴄ (all feminine), (3) verbal nouns ending in ᴀᴄᴄ and ᴀṁᴀⁱɴ, (4) most nouns ending in ᴄ, (5) other nouns ending in consonants which are, as a rule, masculine or feminine, according as they end in broad or slender consonants.

92. The genitive singular is formed by adding ᴀ. If the last vowel of the nom. is ⁱ, preceded by a broad vowel, the ⁱ is usually dropped in the gen., as ᴄoⁱʟ, gen., ᴄoʟᴀ. The vowels of the nom. often undergo a change in the gen. These changes are the *reverse* of the vowel changes in the 1st and 2nd declensions (§ 60.)

Change—

ⁱ, ⁱo or eⁱ (short) in nom. into eᴀ in the gen.
   u or uⁱ   „   „   „ o „   „   „
      éⁱ   „   „   „ éᴀ „   „   „

93. The nominative plural is usually the same as the gen. sing.; but personal nouns ending in óⁱⱼ and éⁱⱼ add í to the nom. sing. to form nom. pl.

96. ### EXAMPLES.

cnáṁ,	cnor,	báoó.ṗ,	buacaill,
a bone.	*a bell.*	*a boat.nan.*	*a boy.*

SINGULAR.

NOM. & ACC.	cnáṁ	cnor	báoóiṗ	buacaill
GEN.	cnáṁa	creara	báoóṗa	buacalla
DAT.	cnáṁ	cnor	báoóiṗ	buacaill
VOC.	a cnáṁ	a cnor	a báoóiṗ	a buacaill

PLURAL.

NOM. & ACC.	cnáṁa	creara	báoóiṗí	buacailli
GEN.	cnáṁ	cnor	báoóiṗ(i)	buacaill(i)
DAT.	cnáṁaiḃ	crearaiḃ	báoóiṗiḃ	buacailliḃ
VOC.	a cnáṁa	a creara	a báoóiṗí	a buacailli

104. The following nouns form their NOMS. PL. by adding nna to the gen. sing. :—am, time ; rrut, a stream ; oṗuim, a back ; giom, a piece ; clear, a trick ; anam, a soul.

Fourth Declension.

106. The fourth declension includes (1) diminutives in ín, (2) most nouns ending in a vowel. All the cases of the singular are alike. The nom. plur. is formed by adding í (if the nom. sing. ends in e the e is dropped).

	SINGULAR.		PLURAL.	
NOM. & ACC.	cailín	cailíní	tigearna	tigearnaí
GEN.	cailín	cailíní	tigearna	tigearnaí
DAT.	cailín	cailíniḃ	tigearna	tigearnaíḃ
VOC.	a cailín	a cailíní	a tigearna	a tigearnaí

113. baile, a town; léine, a shirt; míle, a thousand; teine, a fire; caoi, a method; daoi, a fool; raoi, a wise person; oraoi, a druid; and dlaoi, a curl, make noms. pl., bailte, leinte(aca), mílte, teinte(aca), caoite, daoite, raoite, oraoite, and dlaoite.

Nouns ending in ḋe **or** ġe **take** te **in nom. pl.,** e.g., croiḋe, croiḋte.
The noms. pl. of duine and níḋ are daoine and neite.

The Fifth Declension.

116. Most nouns of this declension end in a vowel, and are, with a few exceptions, feminine. The gen. sing. is usually formed by the addition of n, nn, or c (broad). The dat. sing. is formed by attenuating the gen. § 30, except in those nouns which add c, when the dat. is like the nom. (usually).

119. The nom. pl. is formed (1) by adding a to gen. sing., e.g., peanra, cuirle, and most nouns that form gen. sing. in c; (2) by adding e to gen. sing., accompanied with syncope (§ 33), e.g., gaiḋne, cairḋe, namhḋe, aiḋne, the plurals of gaḃa, cara, namha, and aḃ; (3) by attenuating the gen. sing., e.g., lacain, ficid, caoiris, comunrain.

The gen. pl. is like the gen. sing.

Singular.

Nom. & Acc.	ᵹaba*	capa	cataoıp	éıpe
Gen.	ᵹabann	capaᴅ	cataoıpeac	éıpeann
Dat.	ᵹabaınn	capaıᴅ	cataoıp	éıpınn
Voc.	a ᵹaba	a capa	a cataoıp	a éıpe.

Plural.

Nom. & Acc.	ᵹaıbne	caıpᴅe	cataoıpeaca
Gen.	ᵹabann	capaᴅ	cataoıpeac
Dat.	ᵹaıbnıb	caıpᴅıb	cataoıpeacaıb
Voc.	a ᵹaıbne	a caıpᴅe	a cataoıpeaca

IRREGULAR NOUNS.

132.

	Nom., Acc., Voc.	Gen.	Dat.
Sing.	ataıp, *a father*	atap	ataıp
Plur.	aıtpe, aıtpeaca	aıtpeac	aıtpeacaıb
Sing.	bean, *a woman*	mná	mnaoı
Plur.	mná	ban	mnáıb
Sing.	bó, *a cow*	bó	buın
Plur.	ba	bó	buaıb
Sing.	lá, *a day*	lae	lá, ló
Plur.	laete (anta)	laete, lá	laetıb
Sing.	mí, *a month*	míopa	mí, míp
Plur.	míopa	míop	míopaıb
Sing.	pcıan, *a knife*	pcıne	pcıaın, pcın
Plur.	pceana	pcıan	pceanaıb
Sing.	plıab, *a mountain*	pléıbe	pléıb, plıab
Plur.	pléıbte	pléıbte	pléıbtıb
Sing.	tıᵹ, teac, *a house*	tıᵹe	tıᵹ, teac
Plur.	tıᵹte	tıᵹte, teac	tıᵹtıb
Sing.	Ɗıa, *God.*	Ɗé	Ɗıa.

*In Munster ᵹaba is usually unflected in the *singular.*

mátaıp, bpátaıp, veapbpátaıp, are declined like
ataıp. The gen. of veıpbṗıúp, a sister, is veıpbṗeatap.

After numerals use mí and lá; *e.g*, oċt mí,
ṗé lá.

DECLENSION OF ADJECTIVES.

First Declension.

134. This declension includes all adjectives ending in a broad consonant. The
vowel changes in gen. sing. are the same
as for nouns §§ 60, 78.

Examples.

	móp, *big*		ʒeal, *bright*		vípeaċ, *straight*	
	SINGULAR.					
	MASC.	FEM.	MASC.	FEM.	MASC.	FEM.
N. & Acc.	móp	móp	ʒeal	ʒeal	vípeaċ	víṛ̃aċ
GEN.	móıp	móıpe	ʒıl	ʒıle	vípıʒ	vípıʒe
DAT.	móp	móıp	ʒeal	ʒıl	vípeaċ	vípıʒ
VOC.	móıp	móp	ʒıl	ʒeal	vípıʒ	vípeaċ
	PLURAL.					
N. & Acc.	mópa		ʒeala		vípeaċa	
GEN.	móp		ʒeal		vípeaċ	
DAT.	mópa		ʒeala		vípeaċa	
VOC.	mópa		ʒeala		vípeaċa	

Second Declension.

142. All adjectives ending in a slender
consonant, except those in amaıl, belong
to the second declension.

In the singular all the cases, both masc. and fem., are alike, except the gen. fem., which is formed by adding e.

In the plural all the cases, both masc. and fem., are formed by adding e to the nom. sing., except the gen., which is like the nom. sing.

Example.

mᴀıt, *good.*

	SINGULAR.		PLURAL.
	masc.	fem.	both genders
N. & A.	mᴀıt	mᴀıt	mᴀıte
GEN.	mᴀıt	mᴀıte	mᴀıt
DAT.	mᴀıt	mᴀıt	mᴀıte
VOC.	mᴀıt	mᴀıt	mᴀıte

Third Declension.

146. The third declension includes all adjectives ending in ᴀṁᴀıʟ.

In both numbers the two genders are alike. The gen. sing. and the nom., acc., dat., and voc. pl. are formed by adding ᴀ (with syncope § 33).

Example.

ᚠeᚐᚱᚐᚋᚐᚔᎥ, *manly.*

	SINGULAR.	PLURAL.
N. & A.	ᚠeᚐᚱᚐᚋᚐᚔᎥ	ᚠeᚐᚱᚐᚋᎽᚐ
GEN.	ᚠeᚐᚱᚐᚋᎽᚐ	ᚠeᚐᚱᚐᚋᚐᚔᎥ
DAT.	ᚠeᚐᚱᚐᚋᚐᚔᎥ	ᚠeᚐᚱᚐᚋᎽᚐ
VOC.	ᚠeᚐᚱᚐᚋᚐᚔᎥ	ᚠeᚐᚱᚐᚋᎽᚐ.

Fourth Declension.

148. All adjectives ending in a vowel belong to the fourth declension. They have no inflection; all cases, sing. and plural, are alike.

COMPARISON OF ADJECTIVES.

153. In Irish there are two comparisons (1) the comparison of equality, (2) the comparison of superiority.

The comparison of equality is formed by putting coṁ before the adjective, and ᴌe (or ᴌeᎥᚱ before article) after it. If a *verb* occurs in the second portion of the sentence, ᚐᚷᚒᚱ must be used instead of ᴌe.

Cá Seᚐᚷán coṁ ᴌáᚔᚱᎥᚋ ᴌe Séᚐᚋᚒᚱ. *John is as strong as James.*

Níᴌ ᚱé coṁ ᴌáᚔᚱᎥᚋ ᚐᚷᚒᚱ ᴗí ᚱé. *He is not as strong as he was.*

155. The comparison of superiority has three degrees—the positive, the comparative, and the superlative. **The comparative and superlative have the same form as the genitive singular feminine of the adjective.**

The comparative is usually preceded by níor (ní(ó) + ir), and followed by ná *(than);* if a verb occurs in the second portion of sentence, use ná mar.

Tá an ṡrian níor ṡile ná an ṡealaċ. *The sun is brighter than the moon.* We can also say : ir ṡile an ṡrian ná an ṡealaċ. Tá ré níor láiöre anoir ná mar a bí ré riaṁ. *He is stronger now than ever he was.*

If the comparison is completely past in the mind of the speaker, ní ba is used instead of níor, but if the present time is not completely excluded, níor *may* be used.

Ir óóiċ liom ṡo raib ré níor (ní ba) láiöre ná Seaṡán. *I think that he was stronger than John ;* but, ba óóiċ liom ṡo raib ré ní ba láiöre ná Seaṡán. *I thought that he was stronger than John.*

159. The superlative degree must always be preceded by the verb ir. (ba is used in the past, and baö in the conditional.) *The highest hill in Ireland.* An cnoc ir aoiröe i n-Éirinn

IRREGULAR COMPARATIVES.

POSITIVE	COMP. & SUPER.	POSITIVE	COMP. & SUPER.
beᴀᵹ, *small*	luᵹᴀ	minic, *often*	minicí, mioncᴀ
ꝼᴀᴐᴀ, *long*	ꝼuiᴐe, ꝼiᴀ	ᴄe, *warm*	ᴄeo
móp, *big*	mó	ᴄipim, *dry*	ᴄiopmᴀ
olc, *bad*	meᴀpᴀ	ᵹpánᴐᴀ, *ugly*	ᵹpáinᴐe
mᴀiᴄ, *good*	ꝼeᴀpp	ᴀpᴐ, *high*	ᴀoipᴐe, ᴀipᴐe
ᵹeᴀpp, *short*	ᵹioppᴀ	ᴐóᴄᴀ } *prob-*	{ ᴐóᴄᴀiᴐe
bpeáᵹ, *fine*	bpeáᵹᴄᴀ	ᴐóiᵹ } *able*	{ ᴐóiᵹᴄe.

167. NUMERAL ADJECTIVES.

CARDINALS		ORDINALS	
1.	ᴀon—ᴀṁáin, *or*,—	1st.	céᴀᴐ— (ᴀonṁaᴐ).
2.	ᴐá—	2nd.	ᴐᴀpᴀ—, ᴄᴀpnᴀ—, ᴐóṁaᴐ—
3.	ᴄpí—	3rd.	ᴄpíṁaᴐ—, ᴄpeᴀp—
4.	ceiᴄpe—	4th.	ceᴀᴄpᴀṁaᴐ—
5.	cúiᵹ—	5th.	cúiᵹṁaᴐ—, cúiᵹeᴀᴐ—
6.	pé—	6th.	péṁaᴐ—, peipeᴀᴐ—
7.	peᴀᴄᴄ—	7th.	peᴀᴄᴄṁaᴐ—.
8.	oᴄᴄ—	8th.	oᴄᴄṁaᴐ—
9.	nᴀoi—	9th.	nᴀoṁaᴐ—
10.	ᴐeiᴄ—	10th.	ᴐeiᴄṁaᴐ—, ᴐeᴀᴄṁaᴐ—
11.	ᴀon—ᴐéᴀᵹ.	11th.	ᴀonṁaᴐ—ᴐéᴀᵹ.
12.	ᴐá—ᴐéᴀᵹ.	12th.	ᴐᴀpᴀ—ᴐéᴀᵹ.
13.	ᴄpí—ᴐéᴀᵹ.	13th.	ᴄpíṁaᴐ—ᴐéᴀᵹ.
14.	ceiᴄpe—ᴐéᴀᵹ.	14th.	ceᴀᴄpᴀṁaᴐ—ᴐéᴀᵹ.
15.	cúiᵹ—ᴐéᴀᵹ.	15th.	cúiᵹṁaᴐ—ᴐéᴀᵹ.
16.	pé—ᴐéᴀᵹ.	16th.	péṁaᴐ—ᴐéᴀᵹ.
17.	peᴀᴄᴄ—ᴐéᴀᵹ.	17th.	peᴀᴄᴄṁaᴐ—ᴐéᴀᵹ.
18.	oᴄᴄ—ᴐéᴀᵹ.	18th.	oᴄᴄṁaᴐ—ᴐéᴀᵹ.
19.	nᴀoi—ᴐéᴀᵹ.	19th.	nᴀoṁaᴐ—ᴐéᴀᵹ.
20.	ꝼiᴄe—	20th.	ꝼiᴄṁaᴐ—, ꝼiᴄeᴀᴐ—

CARDINALS—*con.*	ORDINALS—*con.*
21. aon—ir ꝼiċe.	21st. aonṁaṫ—ꝼiċeaḋ (ꝼiċiḋ).
22. ꝺá—ir ꝼiċe.	22nd. ꝺara—ꝼiċeaḋ(ꝼiċiḋ).
30. ꝺeiċ—ir ꝼiċe.	30th. ꝺeiċṁaḋ—ꝼiċeaḋ (ꝼiċiḋ).
31. aon—ꝺéag ir ꝼiċe.	31st. aonṁaḋ—ꝺéag ar ꝼiċiḋ.
40. ꝺaṫaꝺ—, ꝺá ꝼiċiꝺ—	40th. ꝺaṫaꝺṁaḋ—, ꝺá ꝼiċiꝺeaḋ.
50. ꝺeiċ—ir ꝺaṫaꝺ.	50th. ꝺeiċṁaḋ—ir ꝺaṫaꝺ.
60. trí ꝼiċiꝺ—	60th. trí ꝼiċiꝺeaḋ—
70. ꝺeiċ—ir trí ꝼiċiꝺ.	70th. ꝺeiċṁaḋ—ir trí ꝼiċiꝺ.
80. ceiṫre ꝼiċiꝺ—	80th. ceiṫre ꝼiċiꝺeaḋ—
90. ꝺeiċ—ir ceiṫre ꝼiċiꝺ.	90th. ꝺeiċṁaḋ—ir ceiṫre ꝼiċiꝺ.
100. céaꝺ—	100th. céaꝺṁaḋ—
101. —agur céaꝺ.	101st. aonṁaḋ—agur céaꝺ.
102. ꝺá—agur céaꝺ.	102nd. ꝺara—agur céaꝺ.

In the above list the dash indicates the *position* of the noun : thus, aon capall aṁáin, or simply, capall, one horse ; ꝺá capall, two horses ; ꝺá capall ꝺéag, twelve horses. The termination ṁaḋ in the ordinals is pronounced ú (oo). The cardinals may be used in *counting* (without expressing the noun), thus : a h-aon, a ꝺó, a trí, a ceaṫair, a cúig, a ré, a reaċt, a hoċt, a naoi, a ꝺeiċ, a h-aon ꝺéag, a ꝺó ꝺéag, a trí ꝺéag,.........a h-aon ir ꝼiċe, etc. Notice a ꝺó and a ceaṫair.

The Personal Numerals.*

ฺขนฺ1ne	1 person.	ฺขคฺลชฺข (ฺขผ́ ศฺเċเฺข)	
beเฺ́̃ท์	2 persons.	ฺขนฺ1ne	40 persons.
ฺ̃ท์ณฺ́̃ท์	3 „	ฺขนฺ1ne คฺฺ̃̃ทฺ̃ยฺ̃ท ฺขคฺ-	
ceคฺฺ̃̃ทฺคฺ̃ท	4 „	ฺ̃ทคฺ̃ชฺข	41 „
cúเฺ̃̃ทฺฺ̃̃ทฺคฺ̃ท	5 „	ฺขeเฺ̃ท ฺขฺ̃หนฺ1ne	
ฺ̃ทeเฺ̃ทฺคฺ̃ท	6 „	. คฺฺ̃̃ทฺ̃ยฺ̃ท ฺขคฺ̃ชฺข	50 „
móฺ̃ทฺ̃ทeเฺ̃ทฺคฺ̃ท }	7 „	ฺขeเฺ̃tneคฺฺ̃̃หฺ̃ท	
ฺ̃ทeคฺฺฺ̃̃̃ทฺคฺ̃ท }		เฺ̃ท ฺขคฺ̃ชฺข	
õฺฺฺ̃̃ทฺคฺ̃ท	8 „	คoเฺ̃ทne ฺขéคฺฺ̃̃	
nคõฺทฺ̃ทคฺ̃ท	9 „	เฺ̃ท ฺขคฺ̃ชฺข	51 „
ฺขeเฺ̃tneคฺฺ̃̃ทฺคฺ̃ท	10 „	ฺ̃ท์ณ́ ฺขนฺ1ne ฺขéคฺฺ̃̃	
คoเฺ̃ทne ฺขéคฺฺ̃̃	11 „	เฺ̃ท ฺขคฺ̃ชฺข	53 „
ฺขผฺ́̃ทéคฺฺ̃̃	12 „	ฺ̃ท์ณ́ ศฺเċเฺข ฺขนฺ1ne	60 „
ฺ̃ท์ณ́ ฺขนฺ1ne ฺขéคฺฺ̃̃	13 „	ฺขนฺ1ne คฺฺ̃̃ทฺ̃ยฺ̃ท ฺ̃ท์ณ́	
ceเฺฺ̃̃ทe ฺขนฺ1ne		ศฺเċเฺข	61 „
ฺขéคฺฺ̃̃	14 „	beเฺ́̃ท์ เฺ̃ท ฺ̃ท์ณ́	
ฺ̃ทeคฺฺฺ̃̃̃ท ñฺขนฺ1ne		ศฺเċเฺข	62 „
ฺขéคฺฺ̃̃	17 „	céคฺ̃ชฺข ฺขนฺ1ne	100 „
ศฺ̃เċe ฺขนฺ1ne	20 „	ฺขนฺ1ne คฺฺ̃̃ทฺ̃ยฺ̃ท	
ฺขนฺ1ne คฺฺ̃̃ทฺ̃ยฺ̃ท ศฺ̃เċe	21 „	céคฺ̃ชฺข	101 „
beเฺ́̃ท์ เฺ̃ท ศฺ̃เċe	22 „	beเฺ́̃ท์ คฺฺ̃̃ทฺ̃ยฺ̃ท	
ฺ̃ท์ณ́ ฺขนฺ1ne เฺ̃ท ศฺ̃เċe	23 „	céคฺ̃ชฺข	102 „

179. The **Possessive Adjectives** are mo, *my* ; ฺขo, *thy* ; ค, *his,* or *her* ; ผฺ́̃ท, *our* ; ฺขนฺ̃ท, *your* ; ค, *their.* The o of mo and ฺขo is elided before a vowel or ศ : *e.g.,* m'คฺฺ̃̃ทคเฺ̃ท, *my father.* ฺขo usually becomes ฺฺ̃̃ท' before a vowel : *e.g.,* ฺฺ̃̃ท'คฺฺ̃̃ทคเฺ̃ท, *thy father.*

195. The **Demonstrative Adjectives** are ศo (or ศeo), *this* ; ศคn, ศoเฺ̃ท (or ศเฺ̃ท), *that* ; and ซฺ̃ขฺ̃ข, *that* or *yonder.*

---

* From Father O'Leary's mเฺ̃หn-ฺฺ̃̃หเฺ̃ทñฺฺ̃.

The forms in brackets are used after *slender* vowels or slender consonants.

The article must always be used *before* the noun with these adjectives : *e.g.,* ᚐᚅ ᴅᴇᴀɴ ᴘᴏ, *this woman* ; ᚐɴ ꝼᴇᴀꝛ ꝛᴀɴ, *that man* ; ɴᴀ ꝼɪꝛ ꝛᴇᴏ, *these men.*

197. The **Indefinite Adjectives** are ᚐᴏɴ, *any* ; ᴇɪᚷɪɴ(ᴄ), *some, certain* ; ᴇɪᴌᴇ, *other* ; ᴜɪᴌᴇ, *all, whole* ; ᴘᴇ, *whatever* ; and the phrase, ᚐꝛ ᴅɪᴄ, *any at all.*

ᚐᴏɴ and ᴘᴇ precede their nouns, the others follow them. ᚐᴏɴ ᴌᴀ, *any day* ; ᚐɴ ᴅᴜɪɴᴇ ᴇɪᴌᴇ, *the other person.*

201. The **Distributive Adjectives** are ᚷᴀᴄ, ᚷᴀᴄ ᚐᴏɴ, *each* ; ᚷᴀᴄ ꝛᴇ, *every other, every second* ; (ᚐɴ) ᴜɪᴌᴇ, ᚷᴀᴄ ᴜɪᴌᴇ (or ᴄᴜɪᴌᴇ), *every* : ᚷᴀᴄ ᴌᴀ, each day ; ᚐɴ ᴜɪᴌᴇ ꝼᴇᴀꝛ, *every man* ; ᚷᴀᴄ ꝛᴇ ᴍᴅᴌɪᴀᴅᴀɪɴ, *every second year.*

THE PRONOUN.

204. The **Conjunctive Personal Pronouns** * are ᴍᴇ, *I* ; ᴄᴜ, *thou* ; ꝛᴇ, *he* ; ꝛɪ, *she* ; ꝛɪɴɴ, *we* ; ꝛɪᴅ, *you* ; ꝛɪᴀᴅ, *they.*

The **Disjunctive Personal Pronouns*** are ᴍᴇ or ᴍᴇ, *I, me* ; ᴄᴜ (ᴄᴜ), *thou, thee* ; ᴇ, *he, him* ; ɪ, *she, her* ; ꝛɪɴɴ, *we, us* ; ꝛɪᴅ, *you* ; ɪᴀᴅ, *they, them.*

---

* For use of these pronouns refer to Syntax—The Pronoun.

The *emphatic* forms are: mire, *myself;* tura, *thyself;* reirean, *himself;* rire, *herself;* rinne, *ourselves;* rbre, *yourselves;* riaoran, *themselves.*

216. Fifteen of the simple prepositions combine with the personal pronouns to form **Prepositional Pronouns.** The most important of these are the combinations of aʒ, aʃ, ʋo, le, ó, ʃé (ʃaoi), and cun.

aʒ, at, with	aʃ, on	ʋo, to	le, with
aʒam, aṫ me	oʃm, on me	ʋom, me	liom, me
aʒaṫ, ,, thee	oʃt, ,, thee	ʋuit, thee	leaṫ, thee
aiʒe, ,, him	aiʃ, ,, him	ʋo, him	leiʃ, him
aici, ,, her	uiʃċi ,, her	ʋí, her	léi(ċe), her
aʒainn,, us	oʃainn,, us	ʋúinn,us	linn, us
aʒaiḃ,, you	oʃaiḃ ,, you	ʋíḃ you	liḃ, you
acu, ,,them	oʃċa ,,them	ʋóiḃ, them	leo, them

Ó, from.	ʃé, ʃaoi, under	Cun, towards.	
		Connaught.	*Munster.*
uaim	ʃúm	ċuʒam	ċúʒam
uait	ʃúċ	ċuʒaṫ	ċúʒaṫ
uaiʋ	ʃé, ʃaoi	ċuiʒe	ċuiʒe
uaiċi	ʃúiċi	ċuici	ċúiċe
uainn	ʃúinn	ċuʒainn	ċúʒainn
uaiḃ	ʃúiḃ	ċuʒaiḃ	ċúʒaiḃ
uaċa	ʃúċa	ċuca	ċúċa

235. The **Relative Pronouns** are ⍺, *who, which, that;* nⱥc, *who not, which not, etc.;* ꝝo, *that;* ꝑé, cꞮꝝé, ꝝꞮꝝé, *whosoever, whatever;* and ⍺ (causing eclipsis), *what, that which, all that :* e.g., ⱥn ꝑeⱥꞃ nⱥc mꝛeꞮꝛ ⱥnn—*the man who will not be there;* ⱥn ꝛeⱥn ꝝo ꝛꝝuꞮꞁ ⱥn ꝛó ⱥꞮcꞮ—*the woman who has the cow.*

N.B. After a superlative, or any phrase equivalent to a superlative, ꝛⱥ (ꝛⱥꞃ in past tense) is·used for *who, which, that.* ꝛeⱥꞃꝛⱥꝛ ꝛuꞮꞇ ꝝⱥc uꞮꞁe nꞮꝛ ꝛⱥ ꝛꝝuꞮꞁ (or, ꝝⱥc ⱥ ꝛꝝuꞮꞁ) ⱥꝝⱥm—*I shall give you everything that I have.*

238. The **Demonstrative Pronouns** are é (í) ꝝeo, *this;* é (í) ꝝꞮn or ꝝⱥn, *that;* é (í) ꝝꞮꝛ, *that (yonder);* Ɪⱥꝛ ꝝo, *these;* Ɪⱥꝛ ꝝⱥn (ꝝꞮn,) *those;* Ɪⱥꝛ ꝝꞮꝛ, *those (yonder).*

ꝛo ꝛ'é ꝝꞮn Seⱥꝝⱥn. *That was John.* Cé n-Ɪⱥꝛ ꝝo? *Who are these?* ⱥn é ꝝꞮꝛ Comⱥꞃ? *Is that (person yonder) Thomas?* ꝛeⱥnꝛⱥꞮꝛ ꝝⱥn ⱥn ꝝnó. *That will do (the business).*

243. The **Interrogative Pronouns** are cé (cꞮⱥ), *who, which;* cⱥꝛ, cⱥꞮꝛé, céⱥꝛꝛ (cꞃéⱥꝛ), *what;* cé ꞁeꞮꞃ? *whose?* e.g., Cⱥꝛ cⱥ ⱥꝝⱥꞇ? *What have you?* Cé ⱥcu Ɪꞃ ꝝeⱥꞃꝝ? *Which of them is the better?* Cé ꞁeꞮꞃ ⱥn ꞁeⱥꝛⱥꝝ? *Whose is the book?*

THE VERB.

247. In Irish there are two conjugations. They are distinguished by the formation of the future tense. In the first conjugation the 1st pers. sing. of the future ends in ꝼᴀᴅ or ꝼеᴀᴅ, and in the second conjugation it ends in (e)óċᴀᴅ.

Each of the conjugations has three forms (1) the **Synthetic**, (2) the **Analytic**, (3) the **Autonomous.**

249. The synthetic form is that in which the persons are expressed by inflections.

In the analytic there is only one form, and the persons are expressed by means of pronouns.

In the autonomous form the action of the verb is merely expressed, without mentioning the subject.

253. There are *three* moods—the Imperative, the Indicative and the Subjunctive.

The Imperative has only one tense—the present. The Indicative has five tenses— the present, the imperfect, the past, the future, and the conditional (or secondary future). The Subjunctive has two tenses— the present and the past.

261. In both conjugations there are *two sets of terminations*—(1) the broad, (2) the slender. The first set is used with verbs ending in a *broad* consonant; the second with those which end in a slender consonant.

FIRST CONJUGATION.

mol, *praise.*   buaıl, *strike, beat.*

IMPERATIVE MOOD.

	SING.	PLURAL.	SING.	PLURAL.
1st	molaım	{ molaımír { molam	buaılım	{ buaılımír buaıleam
2nd	mol	molaıd (aıgıd)	buaıl	buaılıd (ıgıd)
3rd	molad ré	molaıvír (avaoır)	buaılead ré buaılıvír.	

AUTONOMOUS, moltar.   buaıltear.

INDICATIVE MOOD.

Present Tense.

SING.	PLURAL.	SING.	PLURAL.
molaım	molaımíd	buaılım	buaılımíd
molaıṛ	molann ríb	buaılıṛ	buaıleann ríb
molann ré molaıd		buaıleann ré buaılıd.	

AUTON., moltaṛ.   buaıltear.

RELA-	molannṛ (C.)	buaıleannṛ (C.)
TIVE,	molann (M.)	buaıleann (M.)

Past Tense.

SING.	PLURAL.	SING.	PLURAL.
ṁolar	ṁolamar	buailear	buaileamar
ṁolair(air)	ṁolaḃar	buailir (ir)	buaileaḃar
ṁol ré	ṁolavar	buail ré	buaileavar

AUTON., ṁolaḋ. buaileaḋ.

Imperfect Tense.

ṁolainn	ṁolaimír	buailinn	buailimír
ṁoltá	ṁolaḋ rib	buailteá	buaileaḋ rib
ṁolaḋ ré	ṁolaiḋir	buaileaḋ ré	buailiḋir

AUTON., ṁoltaí. buailtí.

Future Tense.

molꝼaᴅ	molꝼaimíᴅ	buailꝼeaᴅ	buailꝼimíᴅ
molꝼair	molꝼaiᴅ rib	buailꝼir	buailꝼiᴅ rib
molꝼaiᴅ ré molꝼaiᴅ		buailꝼiᴅ ré buailꝼiᴅ	

AUTON., molꝼar. buailꝼear.

RELA- { ṁolꝼar (C.)   buailꝼear (C.)
TIVE { ṁolꝼaiᴅ (M.)   buailꝼaiᴅ (M.)

CONDITIONAL.

ṁolꝼainn	ṁolꝼaimír	buailꝼinn	buailꝼimír
ṁolꝼá	ṁolꝼaᴅ rib	buailꝼeá	buailꝼeaᴅ rib
ṁolꝼaᴅ ré	ṁolꝼaiᴅir	buailꝼeaᴅ ré	buailꝼiᴅir

AUTON., molꝼaí (-ꝼaiᴅe) buailꝼí.

SUBJUNCTIVE MOOD.

Present Tense.

molad	molaimíd	buailead	buailimíd
molair	molaiḋ siḃ	buailir	buailiḋ siḃ
molaiḋ / mola*(M.)	sé molaid	buailiḋ / buaile*(M.)	sé buailid

AUTON., moltar. buailtear.

Past Tense.

molainn	molaimís	buailinn	buailimís
moltá	molaḋ siḃ	buailteá	buaileaḋ siḃ
molaḋ sé	molaidís	buaileaḋ sé	buailidís

AUTON.,	moltaoi.	buailtí.
VERBAL NOUN,	molaḋ.	bualaḋ.
VERBAL ADJECTIVE	moltа.	buailte.

The **Analytic Forms** for the tenses given above are exactly like the forms of the 3rd sing. of the various tenses. The analytic form is *not* used in the 1st per. sing. present tense, and is rarely found in the 1st and 2nd pers. sing. imperfect tense, The second i in the terminations imíd. aimíd, etc., is *not* long in Connaught.

* These are the correct literary forms. They are always used in Munster, except before vowels, when the other form is used (ḋ=g). The forms molaiḋ and buailiḋ are really the older forms of the 3rd sing. present tense indic.

276. The past, the imperfect, and the conditional are usually preceded by the particle ᵼo when no other particle precedes them. In the spoken language ᵼo is often omitted, except when the verb begins with a vowel or ꝼ, or an *unaspirable* consonant. The ᵼo' has become so closely united to the verb, when the latter begins with a vowel, that we frequently find it aspirated, just as if the verb began with this consonant, *e.g.*, níoꝛ ᵼo'ól ꝛé (for níoꝛ ól ꝛé)— *He did not drink.*

The Relative form is the same as the 3rd pers. sing. in all the tenses, except the present and the future (in Connaught).

278. The particle used formerly before the *past tense* was ꝛo. It is now never used by itself, but it occurs in the following compounds :—

Aꝛ, *whether* (an + ꝛo); ᵹuꝛ, *that* (ᵹo + ꝛo); cáꝛ, *where* (cá + ꝛo) ; níoꝛ, *not* ; muꝛaꝛ (or munaꝛ), *unless* ; náꝛ, *that not* ; ᵼáꝛ, *of all those who (whom), to whom* ; leꝛ, *by whom, by which* ; cé'ꝛ, *who was.* (This last form is used *only* with the verb iꝛ.)

282. In the first conjugation the τ in all terminations beginning with this letter is generally *aspirated*, except when the stem ends in one of the consonants, o, n, τ, l, ɼ, c, c, o, ʒ.

SECOND CONJUGATION.

291. The second conjugation comprises (1) derived verbs in ɩʒ or uɩʒ, and (2) syncopated verbs.

293.   **Verbs in ɩʒ.**

bᴀɩlɩʒ, *gather.*   ceᴀnnuɩʒ, *buy.*

Derived verbs in (u)ɩʒ have exactly the same inflections as those of buᴀɩl in all the tenses, except the future and the conditional.

INDICATIVE MOOD.

Future Tense.

SING.	PLURAL.	SING.	PLURAL.
bᴀɩleoċᴀo	bᴀɩleoċᴀɪmío	ceᴀnnóċᴀo	ceᴀnnóċᴀɪmío
bᴀɩleoċᴀɪɼ	bᴀɩleoċᴀɪo ɼɩb	ceᴀnnóċᴀɪɼ	ceᴀnnóċᴀɪo ɼɩb
bᴀɩleoċᴀɪo ɼé	bᴀɩleoċᴀɪo	ceᴀnnóċᴀɪo ɼé	ceᴀnnóċᴀɪo

     Auton., bᴀɩleoċtᴀɲ.   ceᴀnnóċtᴀɲ.

Relative { bᴀɩleoċᴀɼ (C.)   ceᴀnnóċᴀɼ
 { bᴀɩleoċᴀɪo (M.)   ceᴀnnóċᴀɪo.

CONDITIONAL.

baileoċainn	baileoċaimír	ceannóċainn	ceannóċaimír
baileoċtá	baileoċaò rib	ceannóċtá	ceannóċaò rib
baileoċaò ré	baileoċaivir	ceannóċaò ré	ceannóċaivir.

AUTON., baileoċtai (aoi).　　　　ceannóċtai (aoi).

VERBAL NOUN, bailiuġaò.　　　　ceannaċ.

VERBAL ADJECTIVE } bailiġte.　　　ceannuiġte.

SYNCOPATED VERBS.

292. Verbs of *more* than one syllable whose stems end in il, in, iṅ, ir or ing, belong to this class.

　　ruaġaiṅ, *proclaim.*　　coiġil, *spare.*

All the tenses (except future and conditional) of ruaġaiṅ are like those of mol, the stem being ruaġṅ; those of coiġil are like buail, the stem being coiġl. The 3rd sing. past tense is o'ruaġaiṅ ré and coiġil ré : the 2nd sing. imperf., o'ruaġaṅtá and coiġilteá. See Syncope, § 33.

Future Tense.

ꞃuᵃᵹꞃóċᵃꞼ, &c., like ceᵃnnóċᵃꞼ.
coiᵹleoċᵃꞼ, &c., like ꝺᵃileoċᵃꞼ.

Conditional.

ꝺ'ꞃuᵃᵹꞃóċᵃinn, &c., like ceᵃnnóċᵃinn.
coiᵹleoċᵃinn, &c., like ꝺᵃileoċᵃinn.

VERBAL NOUN,	ꞃuᵃᵹᵃiꞃꞇ	coiᵹilꞇ.
VERBAL ADJ.,	ꞃuᵃᵹᵃꞃꞇᵃ	coiᵹilꞇe.

Rules for Formation of Verbal Nouns.

315. (*a*) Verbs of the first conjugation generally form their verbal nouns by the addition of ᵃꝺ or eᵃꝺ; final ı in digraphs and trigraphs is dropped: ꝺún, ꝺúnᵃꝺ; mol, molᵃꝺ; mill, milleᵃꝺ; bꞃiꞃ, bꞃiꞃeᵃꝺ; buᵃil, buᵃlᵃꝺ; ꝺóiᵹ, ꝺóᵹᵃꝺ.

(*b*) Verbs of the second conjugation in iᵹ or uiᵹ form their verbal noun in uᵹᵃꝺ (or ú): ᵃꞃouiᵹ, ᵃꞃouᵹᵃꝺ (or ᵃꞃoú); bᵃiliᵹ, bᵃiliuᵹᵃꝺ (or bᵃiliú); míniᵹ, míniuᵹᵃꝺ (or míniú).

(*c*) Syncopated verbs ending in il, in, or iꞃ, usually form verbal nouns by addition of ꞇ: coꞃᵃin, coꞃᵃinꞇ; ꝺíbiꞃ, ꝺíbiꞃꞇ; lᵃbᵃiꞃ, lᵃbᵃiꞃꞇ; coiᵹil, coiᵹilꞇ.

For exceptions to these rules see Larger Grammar § 316.

IRREGULAR VERBS.

318.   Táim, *I am*.

INDICATIVE MOOD.

	1st	2nd	3rd	Relative	Autonomous
Present.	táim táimío	táir(taoi) tá ré tá ríb * táiu	atá	tátar
		or, tá mé, tá tú, *etc.*			
Habitual.	bím bímío	bír bíonn ríb bío	bíonn ré	bíonn (M.) bíonnr(C.)	bírear
Dependent.	fuilim fuilmío	fuilir fuilti *	fuil ré fuilío	fuil	fuiltear
Past.	bíor bíomar	bír bíobar	bí ré bíouar	bí	bítear
Dependent.	rabar rabamar	rabair rababar	raib ré rabauar	raib	rabtar
Imperfect.	bínn bímír	bíteá bíoú ríb	bíoú ré bíoír	bíoú	bítí
Future.	beaú beimío	beir beió ríb	beió ré beió	(M.)beió	
	(*or*)béaú béimío	béir béió ríb	béió ré béió	(C.)béar	beirear
Conditional.	beinn beimír	beiteá beaú ríb	beaú ré beioír	beaú	
	(*or*)béinn, béiteá, *etc.*			béaú	beirí

* The old termination of the 2nd person plural pres. indic. is still used in : tátaoi, fuilti, veirti, mairti, and (g)cloirti.

SUBJUNCTIVE MOOD.

	1st	2nd	3rd	Autonomous
Present. (ᵹo)	ɼabaᴅ	ɼabaiɼ	ɼaib ɼé	ɼabċaɼ
	ɼábmuiᴅ	ɼaib ɼib	ɼabaiᴅ	

The negative particle for this tense is ná.

Past. (ᵹo m)	binn	biteá	bioᵬ	biċi
	bimiɼ	bioᵬ ɼib	bioiɼ	

The negative particle is náɼ.

Imperative Mood.

bím	bí	bioᵬ ɼé	biteaɼ
bímiɼ	biᵬiᴅ	bioíɼ	

Negative particle is ná.

Verbal Noun : beiċ.

Τáim is the only verb that has a distinct form to express habitual state (or action) in the present tense.

348. The **Dependent Form** of an irregular verb is the form that must be used after the following particles : ní, *not*; an, *whether*; ná or naċ, *that not, whether not*; ᵹo, *that*; cá, *where?*; muɼa (muna), *unless*; ᴅá, *if*; and the relative when governed by a preposition.

333.   1S.

(a) In Principal Sentences.

	Assertive	Interrog.	Negative	Neg. Inter.
Present Tense	ıɼ	ⱥn (b')	ní	naċ (náċ)
Past Tense and Conditional	ba, baö b', ꝺob'	aɼ aɼʙ	níoɼ níoɼʙ	náɼ (1) náɼʙ (2)

	Assertive	Negative
Pres. Subj.	ʒo mba ʒuɼa ʒuɼab	náɼa (1) náɼab (2)
Past Subj.	ꝺá mbaö ꝺá mb'	muɼa (1) muɼab (2)

(b) In Dependent Sentences.

	Assertive	Negative
Present Tense	ʒuɼ (ʒo) ʒuɼab	naċ (náċ) (1) naċ (náċ) (2)
Past	ʒuɼ (ʒo b') ʒuɼʙ	náɼ (1) náɼʙ (2)
Conditional	ʒo mbaö ʒuɼ ʒuɼʙ	naċ mbaö} (1) náɼ náɼʙ (2)

Use lines (1) with consonants, lines (2) with vowels.

342. Stem		Present Tense	Past Tense
Ταbαιη {give. bring.	A.	beiη-ιm; ċuʒ-αιm beiη(eαnn) ηé	ċuʒ-αη
	D.	ταbη-αιm ; ċuʒ-αιm	ċuʒ-αη
Oeιη, *say.*	A.	(α)oeιη-ιm (α)oeιη(eαnn) ηé	oubη-αη (oubαηċ) oubαιηċ ηé
	D.	αbη-αιm, oeιη-ιm	oubη-αη
Fαʒ (ƒαιʒ) {get, ƒáʒ } find.	A.	ʒειb-ιm; ƒαʒ-αιm ʒειb(eαnn) ηé	ƒuαιη-eαη, *or,* ƒuαη-αη ƒuαιη ηé
	D.	ƒαʒ-αιm; ƒáʒ-αιm	ƒuαιη-eαη, *or,* ƒuαη-αη
Oéαn, } do, *make* oéιn {	A.	ʒní-m; oeιn-ιm; ʒní(onn) ηé	ηιnn-eαη, óeιn-eαη ηιnne ηé
	D.	oéαn-αιm oeιn-ιm	oéαηnαη, óeιn-eαη
ƒειc, *see*	A.	ċι-m ; ƒειc-ιm ċí(onn) ηé	ċonnαc-αη (ċonnαc) ċonnαιc ηé
	D.	ƒειc-ιm	ƒ(e)αc-αη (ƒeαcα)
Céιʒ, *go.*	A.	céιʒ-ιm	ċuαó-αη ; ċuαιó ηé
	D.	céιʒ-ιm	oeαċ-αη, oeαʒ-αη, ċuαó-αη
beιη, *carry.* A.&D.		beιη-ιm ; beιη(eαnn) ηé	ηuʒ-αη
ʒαb, *take, go.* A.&D.		ʒαb-αιm	ʒαb-αη
Cloιη, } *hear.* A.&D. cluιn }		cloιη-ιm cluιn-ιm	{ċuαl-αη (ċuαlα), {ċuαlα(ιó) ηé
Cιʒ, ταʒ, } *come.* A. & D. τeαʒ		τιʒ-ιm ; ταʒ-αιm ; τeαʒ-αιm τιʒ(eαnn) ηé	ċánʒ-αη (ċánαʒ) ċáιnιʒ ηé
ιċ, *eat.* A. & D.		ιċ-ιm	o'ιċ-eαη [ouαóαη]

The Imperative mood of the above verbs is formed regularly from the
stem, except cιʒ and oeιη, the 2nd pers. sing. of which are ταη and αbαιη:
the other persons are regular. The Imperfect is formed regularly from

Future Tense	Verbal Noun	Verbal Adjective (Past Participle)
béaṗ-ḟaḋ ; taḃaṗ-ḟaḋ taḃaṗ-ḟaḋ ; tiuḃṗ-aḋ	taḃairt	taḃarta, tugta
(a)ḃéaṗ-ḟaḋ aḃróċ-aḋ	ráḋ	ráiḋte
geoḃ-aḋ, geaḃ-aḋ ḃraiġ·eaḋ, ḃfuiġ-eaḋ	faġáil	faġta faiġte faċta
déan-ḟaḋ ,,	déanaṁ déanaḋ	déanta
ċí-ḟeaḋ, feic-ḟeaḋ feic-ḟeaḋ	feircint feiceál	feicte
raċ-aḋ ; raġ-aḋ ,, ,,	ḋul	[ḋulta]
béaṗ-ḟaḋ	breit	beirte, beirṫa
geoḃ-aḋ; gaḃ-ḟaḋ	gaḃáil	gaḃṫa
cloiṗ-ḟeaḋ cluin-ḟeaḋ	cloiṗint, cloiṗtin cloṗ, cloiṗteál, cluinṗint	cloiṗte cluinte
tioc-ḟaḋ	teaċt	taġta
íoṗ-(ḟ)aḋ	iċe	iṫṫe

the Present Tense stem, and the Conditional from the Future stem. All the other forms are formed quite regularly. Wherever the 3rd pers. sing. presents any difficulty, it is given in the above table.

Defective Verbs.

423. Aꞃ (aꞃꞃ, aꞃꞃa), *says, said*—used only when the exact words of the speaker are given ː aꞃꞃa miꞃe, *said I.*

Ꝺaꞃ, *it seems, it seemed*; ꝺaꞃ liom, *it seems to me, methinks.*

Ꝼeaꝺaꞃ, *I know, I knew*: used only negatively or interrogatively, and inflected as a past tense : ꝼeaꝺaꞃ, ꝼeaꝺaꞃ(iꞃ), ꝼeaꝺaiꞃ ꞃé, etc.

Táꞃla, *it happened, came to pass.*

Ꝺ'ꝼóbaiꞃ, or ba óóbaiꞃ, *it all but happened*; ba óóbaiꞃ ꝺom cuicim, *I had well nigh fallen, I nearly fell.*

435. Interrogative Words and Phrases.

When ? cacain, cé an uaiꞃ | Which (*adj.*) ? cé an . . .
Where ? cá, cé an áic | What ? caꝺ, céaꞃꝺ, cꞃéaꝺ
How ? conuꞃ (cionnuꞃ), cé an caoi | Whither ? cá
Why ? caꝺ na caob (ꝷo), caꝺ cuiꝷe | Whence ? caꝺ aꞃ
How far ? ƚ cé an ꝼaiꝺ. | How much ?ƚ cé méiꝺ, cá
How long ?ƚ an ꝼaꝺa | How many ?ƚ méaꝺ, an'mó
Which (*pron.*) ? cé, cioca, ceoca. | Who ? cé (cia).

All these take the *relative form* of the verb, except cá, caꝺ na caob (ꝷo). caꝺ cuiꝷe (ꝷo), caꝺ aꞃ (ꝷo), which eclipse and take dependent form.

445. ADVERBS.

amac, *out*
amuiꝷ (c), *outside*
ám, ámac, *however*
amƚaiꝺ, *thus, so*
anoct, *to-night*
aꞃ aon coꞃ ƚ *at all*
i n-aon coꞃ
aꞃ éiꝷin, *scarcely*
aꞃ ꝷcúl, *backwards*
anaƚƚ, *hither*
anonn, *thither*
aꞃú* imbáꞃac, *the day after to-morrow*

Adverbs—(continued).

aréir, *last night*

anois, *now*

arís(t), *again*

annsan (sin), *there*

annso, *here*

annsúd, *yonder*

ar ais, *back*

ar ball, *by and by, immediately*

ar dtúis } ar dtús } *at first*

ar maidin, *in the morning*

ar uairib } uaireanta } *sometimes*

anois 7 arís, *now and then*

aníos, *up (from below)*

anuas, *down (from above)*

aniar, *from the West*

aduaid, *from the North*

andeas, *from the South*

anoir, *from the E.*

arú* indé, *the day before yesterday*

anuraid } anuirid } *last year*

beag nác } nác mór } *almost*

ceana, *already*

com faoa'r } an faio } *whilst*

dá rírib, *in earnest*

de ló, *by day*

d'oidce, irr' oidce, *by night*

freisin (leir), *also*

fé (faoi) dó, *twice*

fé (faoi) trí, *thrice*

cora 'n airoe, *at full gallop*

de geit, *suddenly*

ar an dtoirt (go oiaiji), *immediately*

de látair, *presently*

fad ó (roin), *long ago*

faoi deireao (fé deire), *at last, at length*

go deo } go brát(ac) } go léir } go h-iomlán } *for ever, entirely*

go moc, *early*

go luat } go tapaio } *quickly*

go minic, *often*

go h-annam, *seldom*

go fóil, *awhile, yet*

go deimin, *indeed*

i bfao, *far off*

tamall i bfao, *before long*

i gcomnuide, *always*

indé, *yesterday*

indiu, *to-day*

i mbárac } amáireac } *to-morrow*

lá ar n-a bárac, *on the following day*

ar maidin indiu, *this morning*

i mbliaona, *this year*

irteac (motion), *in*

irtig (rest), *inside*

mar an gcéaona, *likewise*

mar rin, *thus*

ó cianaib, *a while ago*

ó (na) céile, *asunder*

ó deas, *southwards*

ó tuaid, *northwards*

ór iriol, *secretly*

ór apo, *openly*

ó roin, *since*

* Arú is usually spelled atrugao, but arú represented the general pronunciation of the word.

Adverbs—(continued).

ριαṁ, *ever*	ρίορ, *down*	um τράċnóna (ρα
ριαρ, *back, west-*	ρυαρ, *up*	τράċnóna), *in the*
wards	ṫαll, *on the other*	*evening*
ροιρ, *eastwards*	*side*	

450.   PREPOSITIONS.

αϩ, *at*	ραοι, ρέ, } *under*	le, *with*
αρ, *on*	ρó (ρά) }	ó, *from*
αρ, *out*	ϩαn, *without*	ροιṁ, ροιm, *before*
ϑαρ, *by* (in swear-	ϩο, *to* (motion)	ṫαρ, ϲαρ, *over*
ing)		
ϑe, *off, from*	ι, α, *in*	ϲρé (ϲρí), ϲρίϑ,
		through
ϑo, *to*	ιοιρ, *between*	um, ιm, *about*

609. The following are employed to translate *English prepositions*: they are followed by the *genitive* case in Irish.

ċun (ċum), *towards*	ι ϑϲαοḃ, *concerning*	αρ ċúl, *behind*
τιmċeαll, *around*	ϑo ρéιρ, *according to*	ι nϑιαιϑ, *after*
ϲρ(e)αρnα, *across*		
(le) coιρ } *beside*	ι meαρϲ, *among*	ϲαρ éιρ, *after* (of time)
le h-αιρ }		
	ι ϩceαnn, *at the end of*	αρ ρυαιϑ, αρ ρυϑ,
oρ coṁαιρ, *before*		*throughout* (of
oρ cιonn, *above*	αρ αϩαιϑ, *opposite*	place)
αρ ρon, *for the sake of*	ι n-αϩαιϑ, *against*	ι n-αιce, *near*
	αρ ρeαϑ, } *dur-*	ι ϩcóιρ, le h-αϩαιϑ,
ι ḃροċαιρ, *along with*	ι ϩcαιτeαṁ, } *ing*	*for* (benefit of
	ι ριτ }	or use of).

451. CONJUNCTIONS.

аċ(τ), *but*   ᴈo, *that*   mᴀp rın ꝼéın, *even*
ᴀᴈur, ır, 7, *and*   nᴀċ, nᴀ, *that...not*   *so*
    ᴈo, nó ᴈo, *until*   munᴀ (munᴀ), *if not,*
ᴀp ᴀ ꝼon ᴈo,   ıoıp...ᴀᴈur, *both*   *unless*
  rıúo ır ᴈo, cé   ...*and*   nᴀ, *than, nor*
  ᴈo, *although*   mᴀ, *if*   nó, *or*
    mᴀp, *as*   ó, *since*
oᴀ, *if*   ꝼé(ᵬ) mᴀp, *accord-*   ó nᴀċ, *since...not*
    ing as   rul, rᴀp, *before*

oe bpıᴈ ᴈo, rᴀoı   ı oτpeo ᴈo ⎫
  náᵬ ır ᴈo, τpᴀ   ᴀp nór ᴈo ⎬ *so that* oᴀ bpıᴈ rın,⎫ *there-*
  'r ᴈo, *because*   ı ᴈcᴀoı ᴈo ⎭   uıme rın ⎬ *fore.*

PART II.

SYNTAX.

The Article.

473. In the following cases the definite article is used in Irish, though not used in English :—

(1) Before surnames, when not preceded by a Christian name : Raıb an bpeatnac ann? *Was Walsh there?*

(2) Before the names of continents, countries, and some cities : An Aıꝼꝑıc, *Africa*; an Spáınn, *Spain*; an Róıṁ, *Rome*; an Aıtne, *Athens*; the genitive case of Ꝁaıllıṁ takes the article. Cataıꝑ na Ꝁaıllṁe, Connoae na Ꝁaıllṁe.

The article is *not* used with Éıꝛe, Alba, and Saꝛana in the NOM., ACC. and DAT. cases.

(3) Before abstract nouns: ᴀɴ ᴄ-oʟc, *evil*; ᴀɴ ᴘeᴀcᴀᴅ, *sin*.

(4) With the demonstrative adjectives: ᴀɴ ꝼeᴀꞃ ꞃo, *this man.*

(5) To translate *"apiece," "per,"* or *"a"* before weights and measures:

    Rᴀoʟ (ꞃeᴀʟ) ᴀɴ ceᴀɴɴ, *sixpence apiece*;

    uᴀıꞃ ꞃᴀ (ınꞃ ᴀɴ) mbʟıᴀᴅᴀın, *once a year.*

(6) With titles which *precede* their noun: ᴀɴ ᴄ-ᴀᴄᴀıꞃ ᴘeᴀᴅᴀꞃ ó ʟᴀoᵹᴀıꞃe, *Father Peter O'Leary.*

(7) To give emphasis: Cuᴀʟᴀ ꞃé ᴀɴ ᴅuıɴe ɴᴀ ᴅıᴀıᴅ, *He heard someone behind him.*

(8) Before the names of classes: Cᴀ́ ɴᴀ ᴅᴀoıɴe ɴíoꞃ ʟᴀıᵹe ɴᴀ́ mᴀꞃ ᴀ ᴅꞃoıꞃ, *People are weaker than they used to be.*

(9) Before the names of the seasons, months, and days of the week, except when they are used in the genitive case as adjectives.

    Aɴ ınᴅıu (or ᴀɴ é ꞃo) ᴀɴ ʟuᴀɴ? *Is this Monday?*

    ınᴅıu ᴀɴ ᴀoıɴe, *To-day is Friday,*

but, lá ṗaṁṗaiṫ, *a summer day*; oiṫċe
ġeiṁṗiṫ, *a winter night*; Ṫé luain, *on
Monday*.

In the following cases the article is used
in English but not in Irish:—

(1) Before a noun followed by a definite
genitive (*i.e.*, the genitive case of a definite
noun): mac an ṗiṗ, *the* son of the man;
ṗeaṗ an ṫiġe, *the* man of the house. When
a demonstrative adj. is used with the first
noun, the article is also used: na ṗocail
úṫ m'aṫaṗ, *those* words of my father.

(2) Before the antecedent of a relative
the article is often omitted: iṗ é ṫuine ṫo
ḃí ann, he is the person who was there.

(3) Before nouns denoting occupation
after proper names: Taṫġ Ṣaṫa, Tim the
smith; Oiṗín Ṗile, Oisin the poet; Coṗmac
báille, Cormac the bailiff.

The Noun.

474. In Irish one noun governs another
in the genitive case: ceann an ċaṗaill, the
horse's head; mac an ṗiṗ, the man's son.

475. Proper names are usually aspirated in the genitive case: peɑnn ṁáɪɲe, Mary's pen; leɑḃɑɲ Ṡeɑʒáɪn, John's book.

477. Apposition has almost entirely disappeared in modern Irish, the second noun being put in the nominative case: ó láɪṁ ɑn ɑtɑɲ peɑoɑɲ ó Lɑoʒɑɪɲe, from the hand of Father Peter O'Leary.

478. A noun used adjectively in English is translated into Irish by the genitive case, and the initial of the genitive is subject to the same rules as regards aspiration and eclipsis, as if it were an adjective: ꝼáɪnne óɪɲ, a gold ring; uḃ cɪɲce, a hen egg.

480. There is no "partitive genitive" in Irish, hence nouns expressing a part of anything are followed by oo or oe with the dative: ɑn cɲɑoḃ ɪꝛ ɑoɪɲoe oe'n cɲɑnn, the highest branch of the tree; cuɪo ooꝛ nɑ (oe nɑ) ꝼeɑɲɑɪḃ, some of the men.

481. The personal numerals (§ 177) take the article in the singular, and the noun after them in the genitive plural, except when they are used partitively—in this case they take ᴅo or ᴅe with the dative: ᴀn cúiᵹeᴀṛ ṛeᴀṛ, the five men; ᴀn ᴅeiṛᴄ ṁᴀc, the two sons; nᴀonᴅᴀṛ ᴅoṛ nᴀ ṛeᴀṛᴀiᴅ, nine of the men.

484. A Christian name, when used in addressing a person, is always in the vocative case, preceded by ᴀ : ṛᴀn ᴌiom, ᴀ Ṡeᴀmᴀiṛ, Wait for me, James.

486. Surnames, when not preceded by a christian name, usually take the termination −ᴀċ, and are then declined like mᴀṛcᴀċ (§ 57); or mᴀc may be used before Uí (the genitive of Ó): ᴅṛuiᴌ ᴀn ṗᴀoṛᴀċ ᴀnnṛo ? Is Power here ?; Cᴀṗᴀᴌᴌ ᴀn Ḃṛiᴀn-ᴀiᵹ, O'Brien's horse; ᵹᴀᴅ i ᴌeiᴄ, ᴀ ṁic Uí Ċᴀoiṁ, Come here, O'Keeffe.

488. A surname preceded by any of the words Ó, Uᴀ (fem., Ṅí), or mᴀc (fem., Ṅic), is put in the genitive case. It is aspirated after Ṅí or Ṅic, also after Uí and ṁic (the genitives of Ó and mᴀc). Seᴀᵹán Ó Connᴀiᴌᴌ, John O'Connell ; mᴀiṛe Ṅí Ċonnᴀiᴌᴌ, Mary O'Connell ; ᴌeᴀᴅᴀṛ Ṡeᴀᵹáin Uí Ċonnᴀiᴌᴌ, John O'Connell's book.

The Adjective.

494. As a general rule the adjective follows the noun it qualifies : ꝼeaꝛ maıꞇ, a good man ; leaꝺaꝛ móꝛ, a big book.

Numeral adjs. consisting of one word, possessive and interrogative adjectives precede their nouns.

495. When an adjective *follows* the noun it qualifies, it agrees with the noun in gender, number and case : beaɴ móꝛ, a big woman ; mac aɴ ꝼıꝛ móıꝛ, the son of the big man ; ɴa ꝼıꝛ móꝛa, the big men.

496. Whenever an adjective is predicated of a noun by any verb, the adjective never agrees with the noun, and is not inflected for gender or number : ꞇá aɴ ꝼeaꝛ ꝛaɴ láıꝺıꝛ, that man is strong ; ꞇá ɴa ꝼıꝛ ꝛıɴ láıꝺıꝛ, those men are strong.

499. Adjectives denoting fulness or a part of anything, are followed by ꝺe with the dative : bí aɴ baꝛaıle láɴ ꝺ'uıꝛce, the barrel was full of water.

505. The **Numeral Adjectives** aoɴ, ꝺá, ceaꝺ (*first*), and ꞇꝛeaꝛ cause aspiration ;

if the noun begins with ꞃ, ᴀon prefixes ꞇ
(§ 28) : ᴀn ᴄéᴀᴅ ꞃeᴀꞃ, the first man ; ᴅᴀ
ᴄᴀpᴀll, two horses.

507. Seᴀᴄꞇ, oᴄꞇ, nᴀoı, ᴅeıᴄ, and their
compounds cause eclipsis, and prefix n to
vowels : ꞃeᴀᴄꞇ mᴅᴀ, seven cows ; ᴅeıᴄ
n-uᴅlᴀ, ten apples.

508. ꞇꞃí, ceıꞇꞃe, ᴄúıꞃ, ꞃé aspirate ᴄéᴀᴅ,
100, and míle, 1,000, and may or may not
aspirate other words; **they eclipse all nouns
in the Gen. Pl.** ; ꞇꞃí ᴄéᴀᴅ, 300 ; ceıꞇꞃe
míle, 4,000 ; luᴀᴄ ꞇꞃí ᴅpúnꞇ, £3 worth.

509. The noun after ᴀon, ꞃıᴄe, ᴅᴀꞇᴀᴅ
(ᴅᴀ ꞃıᴄıᴅ), ꞇꞃí ꞃıᴄıᴅ, ceıꞇꞃe ꞃıᴄıᴅ, ᴄéᴀᴅ
and míle is always in the singular: ᴀon
uᴅᴀll ᴅéᴀꞃ, eleven apples ; ꞃıᴄe ᴄᴀpᴀll,
twenty horses. The other numerals (except ᴅᴀ) may take the singular number,
when unity of idea is expressed ᴅeᴀꞃmuıᴅ
ꞃé nᴀ ꞇꞃí ᴅuılle ᴅo ᴅuᴀlᴀᴅ. He forgot to
strike the three blows.

514. The noun after ᴅᴀ, *two*, is always
in the **Dual Number,** which in every Irish
noun has the same *form* as the dative

* There are *three* numbers in Irish:—the Singular, the Dual,
and the Plural.

singular. All the cases of the dual number are alike, but the form of the genitive plural is often used for the genitive dual: ⱱᴀ́ ċᴀpᴀʟʟ, two horses; ⱱᴀ́ ʟᴀ́ɱ, two hands; ⱱᴀ́ ⱱuın (ⱱᴀ́ ⱱó), two cows.

524. The **Possessive Adjectives** are usually followed by the word cuıⱱ when we wish to express the portion of a thing or of a class of things which belongs to one or more persons : mo cuıⱱ ᴀⱤᴀ́ın, my bread ; ᴀ cuıⱱ ꝼíonᴀ, his wine ; ᴀ cuıⱱ ʟeᴀⱱᴀⱤ, her books ; ᴀ ᵹcuıⱱ cᴀpᴀʟʟ, their horses.

We often use the definite article in Irish where the possessive adjectives would be used in English : ConuⱤ ᴀ ⱱꝼuıʟ ᴀn cⱤʟᴀ́ınce ? How is *your* health ? ; nᴀ́ Ɽᴀnncuıᵹ cuıⱱ nᴀ comuⱤⱤᴀn, do not covet *your* neighbour's goods ; ConuⱤ ᴀcᴀ́ ᴀn cúⱤᴀm ? How is *your* family ?

The Pronoun.

528. The **Personal Pronouns** agree with the nouns for which they stand in number and person, but not always in gender. If the gender of a noun be different from the

sex of the person denoted by the noun, the
pronoun agrees in gender with the sex:
ιr mαιτ αn cαιlín (*m.*) í.   She is a good
girl. ιr οιc αn coṁuρρα (*f.*) é. He is a
bad neighbour. ιr ραιοὁιη αn ρcοιός (*f.*)
é.   He is a rich farmer.

532. The personal pronouns always come
after the verb: moιαnn ρé τú, he praises
you.

209. The **Conjunctive forms of the personal pronouns are used only immediately
after the verb as its subject; in all other
positions the Disjunctive forms must be
used.** The disjunctive forms are used with
ιr, because the word immediately after ιr
is *never* the subject (see § 589).

535. The accusative pronoun usually
comes last in the sentence or clause to
which it belongs: ο'ϝάς ρé ραn άιτ ριn é.
He left it in that place.

538. The **Relative Pronoun** when governed by a preposition causes eclipsis,
except in the past tense (with regular
verbs). In the past tense (regular verbs)
it unites with ηo, the old particle used

with this tense, and becomes ᴀᴦ: ᴀɴ ᴀ́ɪᴄ ɪ n-ᴀ ('nᴀ) ḃᴼᴜɪʟ ᴦᴇ́, the place in which he is; ᴀɴ ᴦᴇᴀᴦ ᴅ'ᴀᴦ ᵹᴇᴀʟʟᴀᴦ mo ʟᴇᴀḃᴀᴦ, the man to whom I promised my book.

541. In colloquial Irish the last phrases and similar ones are translated thus: ᴀɴ ᴀ́ɪᴄ ᵹo ḃᴼᴜɪʟ ᴦᴇ́ ᴀɴɴ; ᴀɴ ᴦᴇᴀᴦ ᵹᴜᴦ (or ᴀᴦ) ᵹᴇᴀʟʟᴀᴦ mo ʟᴇᴀḃᴀᴦ ᴅᴼ. Ann and ᴅᴼ are *prepositional pronouns*, not simple prepositions. Compare the following: ᴀɴ ḃᴇᴀɴ ᵹo ḃᴼᴜɪʟ ᴀɴ ḃᴼ ᴀɪᴄɪ (or, ᴀɴ ḃᴇᴀɴ ᴀᵹ ᴀ ḃᴼᴜɪʟ ᴀɴ ḃᴼ), the woman who has the cow.

555. The relative is distinctly marked by the position of the words:

Ꞇᴀ́ ᴀɴ ᴦᴇᴀᴦ ᴀᵹ oḃᴀɪᴦ. The man is at work.

Ꭺɴ ᴦᴇᴀᴦ ᴀᴄᴀ́ ᴀᵹ oḃᴀɪᴦ. The man who is at work.

The Verb.

547. As a general rule the verb precedes its subject: ᴄᴀ́ ᴦᴇ́, he is; ḃɪ ᴀɴ ᴦᴇᴀᴦ ᴀɴɴ, the man was there.

548. Transitive verbs govern the accusative case, and the usual order of words is —Verb, Subject, Object : ḃuaıl an ⱜeaⱜ ⱜan é, that man struck him.

For the conditions under which a verb is aspirated or eclipsed see § 21 (*g*) and § 26 (*e*).

549. The most frequent use of the subjunctive mood is with the conjunction ⰷo (negative naⱜ), to express a wish :

ⰷo mḃeannuıⰷıⱜó Oıa óuıⱅ ! May God bless you !

ⰷo maıⱜıⱜó aⱜ nⰷaeluınn ⱜlán ! May our Irish Language prosper !

561. In Irish there is neither an infinitive mood nor a present participle, both functions being discharged by the verbal noun. When the verbal noun is preceded by the preposition aⰷ (or a') it is equivalent to the English present participle. The verbal noun governs the noun immediately after it in the genitive case.

Ⱅá ⱜé a' óul aḃaıle, He is going home. Ⱅá ⱜıaó a' ⱅeaċⱅ, They are coming. Ⱅá na páıⱜóí aⰷ ımıⱜⱅ, The children are playing.

Ḃí sé a' baint an féir. He was cutting the grass. Tá an fear ġá ḃualaḋ. The man is striking him.

When the English present participle expresses *rest, e.g., standing, sitting, lying, sleeping, etc.*, we must use the preposition i (*in*) compounded with a suitable possessive adjective : Tá mé am ('mo) ċoḋlaḋ, I am asleep; tá sé 'na ṡuiḋe, He is sitting; ḃí an ḃean na seasaṁ ag an doras. The woman was standing at the door.

566. The infinitive of an English intransitive verb is translated by the simple verbal noun. Duḃairt sé liom dul go Corcaiġ, He told me to go to Cork. Is fearr liom siuḃal, I prefer to walk.

568. The infinitive of a transitive verb (no purpose implied) is translated by the verbal noun preceded by the preposition do (or a). **Note the order of the words.** Duḃairt m'aṫair liom capall do ċeannaċ, My father told me to buy a horse. Ba ċóir duit an féar a ḃaint, You ought to have cut the grass.

569. When the English infinitive expresses purpose use ᴛe before the verbal noun if the infinitive is intransitive, otherwise use ċun or ᴛe before the object of the English infinitive, and ᴅo or ᴀ before the verbal noun.

Ċáinɪᵹ ɼé ᴛe ꝼᴀnᴀṁᴀɪnᴛ, He came to stay.

Ċuᴀɼᴅ ɼé ċun ᴀn ᴅoɼᴀɪɼ ᴀ ᴅúnᴀᴅ, He went to shut the door.

Ċáinɪᵹ ɼé ᴛeɪɼ ᴀn ᵹcᴀpᴀʟʟ ᴅo ċeᴀnnᴀċ, He came to buy the horse.

Ꝺ'éɪɼɪᵹ ɼé nᴀ ꝼeᴀɼᴀṁ ċun nᴀ ᴠꝼeᴀɼ ᴅo ᴠuᴀʟᴀᴅ, He stood up to strike the men.

The following construction is frequently used :

Ċáinɪᵹ ɼé ᴀᵹ ᴅíoʟ ᴀn ċᴀpᴀɪʟʟ, He came to sell the horse.

580. "Not" before an English infinitive is translated by the preposition ᵹᴀn :

Ꝺuᴠᴀɼᴛ ʟeɪɼ ᵹᴀn ᴀn ᴅoɼᴀɼ ᴀ ᴅúnᴀᴅ, I told him *not* to shut the door.

Ꝁᴅᴀɪɼ ʟe ᴠɼɪᴀn ᵹᴀn ᴀn ᵹoɼᴛ ᴅo ᴛɼeᴀᴠᴀᴅ, Tell Brian *not* to plough the field.

The Verb ıS.

588. The verb ıꞃ must be used

(1) When we tell or ask *who* (or *which*) a person (or thing) is or was. (Sentences of identity.)

(2) When we tell or ask *what* a person or thing is or was, *without any reference to his or its becoming so.* (Sentences of classification.)

(3) When we wish to *emphasize* any idea other than that contained in the verb.

EXAMPLES.

Who? or **Which?**	John is the man,	ıꞃ é Seaᵹán an ꝼeaꞃ.
	James is my brother,	ıꞃ é Séamaꞃ mo ꝺeaꞃbꞃátaıꞃ.
	Is that your book?	An é ꞅın ꝺo leaꝑaꞃ ?
	That is the white horse,	ıꞃ é ꞅın an capall bán.

Notice the use of the personal pronoun between ıꞃ and a definite noun.

ıꞃ é is pronounced, and usually written, 'ꞃé; similarly 'ꞃí, and 'ꞃıaꝺ.

58

What?	John is a priest.	ᵼᵼ ᵼᵅᵹᵅᵽᵼ Seᵅᵹᵅᴎ.
	Dermot was a king.	ᵬᵅ ᵽᵼ ᴆᵼᵅᵽᵐᵁᵼᴆ.
	A cow is an animal.	ᵼᵼ ᵅᵼᵯᵐᵼᴆᵉ ᵬᴏ́
	A salmon is a fish.	ᵼᵼ ᵼᵅᵽᵼ ᵬᵽᵅᴆᵅᴎ.

Emphasis.	We went to Derry *yesterday*.	ᵼᵼ ᵐᴆᵉ́ ᴆᴏ ᵼᵁᵅᵐᵅᵽ ᵹᴏ ᴆᴏᵼᵽᵉ.
	We went to *Derry* yesterday.	ᵼᵼ ᵹᴏ ᴆᴏᵼᵽᵉ ᴆᴏ ᵼᵁᵅᵐᵅᵽ ᵐᴆᵉ́.
	He is *sick*.	ᵼᵼ ᵼᵼᴎᴎ ᵅᵼᵅ́ ᵼᵉ́.
	He has the money.	ᵼᵼ ᵅᵼᵹᵉ ᵅᵼᵅ́ ᵅᴎ ᵼ-ᵅᵼᵽᵹᵉᵅᴆ.

In the first set of examples it will be noticed that the English subject comes immediately after ᵼᵼ, whilst in the second set the English subject comes last in Irish.

Every sentence must contain, at least, two things—a *subject*, and a *predicate*. Whatever we are speaking about is called the subject ; whatever information we give (or seek) about the subject is the predicate. In the case of transitive verbs in the active voice we must also have an *object* to complete the idea.

589. The verb ᴉꞃ must be immediately followed by the predicate of the sentence. There is no exception to this rule.

EXAMPLES.

An eagle is a bird.	ᴉꞃ éan (ꝼ)ᴉоᴌaꝛ.
Is that a book?	Aꞃ ᴌeaᴅaꝛ é ꞃᴉn ?
Tim is a farmer.	ᴉꞃ ꞃcoᴌóꞡ Ꞇaᴅꞡ.
Is it a ghost ?	Aꞃ ꞇaᴉóᴅꞃe é ?
It is a cow.	ᴉꞃ ᴅó í.
John is a doctor.	ᴉꞃ ᴅocꞇúᴉꞃ Seaꞡán.
Roderick was a king.	ᴅa ꞃí Ꞃuaᴉóꞃí.
Turf is not coal.	ní ꞡuaᴌ móᴉn.
Coal is not turf.	ní móᴉn ꞡuaᴌ.
Water is not milk.	ní ᴅaᴍne uᴉꞃce.

590. In sentences of identity (§ 588 (1)) there is a great difference between English and Irish construction. **In Irish the more particular and individual of the two nouns (or pronouns) is made the predicate,** in English it is made the subject. The following will exemplify.

Q. Who are you?	A. I am the messenger.
Q. Who is the messenger?	A. I am the messenger.
Q. Who was Roderick O'Connor?	A. Roderick O'Connor was the last ᴀɼ'ᴏ-ɲí of Ireland.
Q. Who was the last ᴀɼ'ᴏ-ɲí?	A. Roderick O'Connor was the last ᴀɼ'ᴏ-ɲí.

These answers show the tendency in English of making the more particular or individual of the two the *subject.* In Irish it is made the *predicate.*

(*a*) A proper noun is more individual than a common noun.

(*b*) A pronoun of the first or second person is more individual than a pronoun of the third person.

(*c*) A pronoun of the first or second person is more individual than a proper or a common noun.

(*d*) A pronoun of the third person, *unless when it is equivalent to a demonstrative pronoun,* is *not* more individual than a noun.

Examples.

Con is the king.	'Sé Conn an ꞃí.
You are the man.	Iꞅ ꞇuꞃa an ꞃeaꞃ.
I am the messenger.	Iꞅ miꞅe an ꞇeaꞇꞇaiꞃe
I am he.	Iꞅ miꞅe é.
You are John.	Iꞅ ꞇuꞃa Seaᵹán.
Erin is our country.	'Sí Éiꞃe aꞃ oꞇíꞃ.
Irish is our language.	'Sí an Ᵹaeluinᵹ (Ᵹaeoilᵹe) aꞃ oꞇeanᵹa.
Are you Mary?	An ꞇuꞃa Máiꞃe?
James is the man of the house.	'Sé Séamaꞅ ꞃeaꞃ an ꞇiᵹe.
He is my father.	'Sé ꞃin m'aꞇaiꞃ.
It is the master.	'Sé an maiᵹiꞅꞇiꞃ é.
It is my friend.	'Sé mo caꞃa é.

In the above sentences the underlined words are the predicates.

In § 588 (2) the words " *without any refer-ence to his or its becoming so* " are very important : because if there be any idea of *change of state* in the mind, we *cannot* use the verb ꞇ. If we wish to convey the idea

that a person or thing *has become* what he
(or it) is, *and that he (or it) was not always so,*
we must use the verb τά. **In such con-
structions the verb τά must be always
followed by the preposition ⁊ (in) and a
suitable possessive adjective.**

Τá ρé ⁊n' (⁊nᴀ) ϝeᴀρ, He is a man (*i.e.,*
no longer a boy). ⁊ρ ϝeᴀρ é, He is a man
(*i.e.,* not a woman or a ghost). Τá ρí 'nᴀ
mnᴀoⁱ ṁóⁱρ ᴀnoⁱρ, She is a big woman now.
Ḃϝuⁱl τú ᴀᴅ ḃuᴀcᴀⁱll ṁᴀⁱτ? Are you a
good boy? Ḃí ᴀᴅ cᴀⁱlín ṁᴀⁱτ, Be a good
girl.

Printed in the USA
CPSIA information can be obtained
at www.ICGtesting.com
LVHW011341061023
760261LV00005B/254

9 781015 623125